Sometimes She Talks to Crows

Sometimes She Talks to Crows

Poems by

Alice Lee

Best,

ALee

Kelsay Books

Cover Photograph: Samuel Zeller on Unsplash
Back Cover Photograph: Wayne Lee

ISBN: 13-978-1-947465-25-1

Kelsay Books
Aldrich Press
www.kelsaybooks.com

To all my girls, strong, kind and brave

Acknowledgments

Thanks to the editors of the following small presses and magazines in which these poems previously appeared. Before 1995 I was known as Cheryl Morse, so some of the poems have this earlier name. Special thanks to the editor of Barranca Press who published my memoir in 2015, *Necklace of Stones: A Memoir of Poetry and Place.*

"At the Oceanview Cemetery in Port Angeles" *Adobe Walls,* Albuquerque, NM.

"Classic Red" *Albuquerque Rides Bus Project.*

"Waiting for Annie" *Alaska Poetry Review; Orca Press Broadside.*

"Abalone Woman Experiments" *Calyx, A Journal of Art and Literature by Women,* Corvallis, OR.

"Seaplane," "Nightwave," "Shi Yan (Stone Mountain)," "The Disappearing Gardener," "The Breadman's Daughter," "Letter to my Sister," "Poem in my Husband's Notebook," "Sneaking Past the Guards at the Gate of Bei Wei," "Red," "Wind," "The Things She Left," "This Message," "Gift from Port Townsend" and "Women Picking Blackberries" *Necklace of Stones: A Memoir of Poetry and Place,* Alice Lee, Barranca Press, Taos, NM.

"The Disappearing Gardener" shortlisted for Great Britain's Bridport Prize.

"Red," "Wind," "Sneaking Past the Guards at the Gate of Bei Wei," "Slender Joy," "This Message," "Bamboo in the Moonlight," "Night Watch, Mid-Autumn" and "The Disappearing Gardener," *China Moon,* "Alice Lee," Finishing Line Press.

"Wind" *Mary Tallmountain Tribute,* San Francisco, CA.

"Seaplane" *New Mexico Poetry Review.*

"Gift from Port Townsend," "The DH Lawrence Tree," "Orca Inlet," "Last Day in Town" and "Fox Dream" *Orca Anthology of Poetry and Prose,* Orca Press, Sitka, AK.

"If I Let Myself" *Seattle Public Bus Project.*

 "Night Watch, Mid-Autumn" and "If I Let Myself" *Twenty Poems from the Blue House,* Alice Morse Lee and Wayne Lee, Whistle Lake Press, Anacortes, WA.

"Don't Move" *Windfall,* Portland, OR.

Contents

Also by Alice Lee:

Necklace of Stones: A Memoir of Poetry and Place
China Moon
Twenty Poems from the Blue House (with Wayne Lee)

I. Alaska

I saw what I saw with clarity. But I didn't know
what I was looking at.
> —VS Naipaul, *The Enigma of Arrival*

Sometimes She Talks to Crows

1.
My husband's wedding ring, gone;
he removed it and laid it
on the picnic table near
Signature Rock
in central New Mexico; it disappeared.
Crow? Squirrel? Two-legged human?
We'll never know for sure,
but we like to think it was carried off
by a corvid to be placed in its nest as a prize,
a shiny bauble in the tall pine above us.
Ringless, he finds a Zuni wedding band
in the thrift store—for two bucks.

2.
Crows are smarter than we give them credit for.
Wiley, highly adaptable, they survive
in urban areas, along with pigeons,
who are not as smart; look at their brain size.
I know, in the wars there were carrier pigeons,
but how much intelligence did that take?

In Seattle there is a young girl who talks to crows,
and gives them gifts—a piece of foil,
coins, Cracker Jack rings....
If the crows look long and hard enough
they might find her a tiara in return.

3.
In Southeast Alaska my environmental boss
finds a dead raven on Katlian Street
near the Pioneer Bar. He takes it home

and places it in his freezer. Why? you ask.
Is he going to perform an avian autopsy?
Have it stuffed with piercing glass eyes?
Or give this mysterious bird a decent burial?

4.
Silence, a walk through an urban park,
then I hear ravens everywhere,
competing with their cousins, crows
and screeching eagles cavorting
high in the updrafts.
Plumber's drip, plop, plop, they mimic.
They are shameless, hopping around,
flying off at the last minute
from picking at road kill,
pecking out eyes, feeding on guts.

5.
On our daily walk we see
and hear crow commotion;
a fledgling has fallen out of its nest.
The parents are visibly upset.
Oscar, the groundskeeper and fix-it man,
entreats us to stay back,
has his son climb the tree
to upright the fallen nest,
and quietly in Spanish
he tells the son to carefully
put the baby bird back.

Night Wave

In winter you write
I don't know where we are.

We wake to the sound of rain,
Look for salvation.
We climb out of the ancient volcano
And stand, two mute windows
In a tall white house.
Imbedded in our skin we find
Bits of green glass.
We are the bitter center of the apricot.
Tomorrow we leave this cold climate.
We, fine pieces of winter—slivers of ice—
We break, we melt.
Disappear only to reappear as
Thin birdsong in faraway trees.
Leave silver stars behind.

We enter a country of no return.
We enter and find that which was
Always beckoning, always there.

Raven Returns

Watching the air fill with snow
I stand at the window talking
to you. Through white space
raven wings appear.

From behind the hemlock
Raven sits and watches,
flies to another perch,
watches from three angles.
Spy.

It's a brief storm;
the other side of the snow cloud
shows blue.

You are gone.

I step outside and hear
the laughter in the trees.

Hunting and Gathering

Salmonberry voices—
four women weave and wind
through berry bushes,
thistles, summer sea grass.
Their talk is wind-blown.
The words group in islands
against the breaking of the waves.

Now it is that time
in such a place as this
when all summer light
gathers in one great ball
until it sinks behind the horizon.
And the women and all
slow down to the winter night
to sleep, to wait, to come again.

Fire, Dance, Tree

Stack the cordwood
heartwood,
for the coming cold.

Scatter light over winter.

Fire dance,

dance in the dark, fire of dreams.

In tree air, fire warms
my woman body—a word, a motion—
fire in me.

Eyecatcher,
tree,
turn to cloud, ash, wind.

Against a starry night, tree—
stark, on top of a hill.
Naked place.

Sounds of summer insects at night.
The screened-in porch, children asleep.

This dying in a cold world—
light of the wind and tree.
Music of summer—
stay, long light, stay.

Abalone Woman Experiments

Abalone woman mixes
Fire   water   air
Sings: *In a swimming white house the green girl goes.*

She weaves night through dawn;
Black white   black white
Long fingers remember the pattern.
A few strokes, this is the sign for tides.
Mark the time. Wait, turn, wait.
And this, the salmonberry, red triangular motion,
Over bramble, under branch, at the cannery in the rain.
And since this is the time for spawning salmon,
She finishes the edges in a deepening red—fins.

Abalone woman mixes
Salt water with the rain.
Repeats: *In a swimming white house the green girl goes.*

Under water the colors blend to make a sky of blue,
Then fades back to green again, shaping. This is for the edge.
The shell used for this. Scallop the edge and then make smooth.
Inside the mussel it is deep blue.
Alive and waiting for the summer tides.

In three days she has the formula down for islands.

They claim that woman
Who lives on top of the mountain
Can make the rain with no problem.
But getting it to stop is another story.

In Praise of the Wilderness Rainforest

Night of no clouds
the island dreams
under a silver sky.

Ten islands,
small tree furred
whales.

Mountains
blue and
approaching.

Raven
visits on a Sunday
summer morning.

Cedars in the high fog
red berries
in the graveyard.

Wild roses
whisper
rain.

Fox Dream

The foxes are on the move
Now goes the moon
Tumbling through the half-hole
There will be many foxes
Traveling white on white
Over moonlit paths
While owl blinks twice
In the blackest night
Like an eye in the sky
Like the half-hidden moon

Leaving a Friend

It is the last afternoon
and I must take out the old salmon
to the crows on the beach
before I say goodbye.
Down a hundred steps
through grey rain and smoke
to the rocky shoreline,
I scatter the fish.

Wind slides along the sea of your house.
I remember to throw out the first-day flowers.
And I make sure the door latch
is secured from the wind.

Skeleton in the Weeds

Peel the apples, throw the cake in the oven,
pack school lunches, all the while
musing over past betrayals,
tight knot in shoulders,
sleep alone, dream of cats
giving birth to large litters.

Heart energy stored up, fermenting
ideas drift like wild dandelion fluff—
seeded. They are vagrant weeds
in someone else's yard.

A few bones, smooth and cool to the finger's touch
These bones push up under late green May covering—
flayed violets.

Pretend the world still makes magic.
A small ivory song invades. Necessary.
Morning hours stolen.
Quiet comes.

Seaplane

By now the Alaskan bush pilot
recognizes me, calls me by first name.
The Cessna floatplane
rises out of the channel waters,
Sitka Sound,
an awkward pterodactyl.

I head toward
the Indian fishing village
across the mountains.
Yellow plane squeaks through
so close I see fissures,
white on white.

He waits on the dock,
smoking a cigarette,
my good-for-nothing lover—
blue shirt,
black hair,
sunglasses,
cowboy boots.
He flicks his cigarette in the bay.

The plane drops out of the clouds,
taxis through
the silver water,
an arc of bright desire.

The DH Lawrence Tree

Saints, I tell you, the world is mad.

It wants back its trees
and birdsong—individual notes,
so tiny and pure,
so musical, musical.

In New Mexico there is a tree,
the DH Lawrence tree,
made famous by an O'Keeffe painting.

Night,
lying under the spreading tree,
stars spin out, slowly revolving
from the powerful, twisted limbs.

Night of starless sleep,
this tree comes to me, the dream
of a powerless, peace-filled world,
slowly revolving.

In Southeast Alaska, pulp mill town,
rain spills out of August—
eleven inches in 23 days—
and the cedars and hemlocks
spiral into the stars.

Lying under the massive hemlock
next to my small house,
a bird speaks in musical notes.

How we talk to one another,
how we remember the way it used to be;
take in the comfortable silence.

Living by the Heart

Dark side of the moon,
there was never a time
you were not a strange, aching memory.

From anonymous room,
empty and white,
I come to you, across water, across time,
to find your red geometric house
cornered in a forest of hemlocks
behind swamp of cedar.

Under your heart I find
slips of answers, none complete,
and settle for what little I know.

Filling up silence back in these woods,
this is the way of hemlock living—
a tree dancer
          small white flowers at tideline
                    fog settling over the mudflats.

A wooden flower—this house of yours—
with trap doors, spinning windows,
the type that will implode someday
from within.
          Covered by the blue forest light,
                    we adopt rain
and watch the wood smoke drift by the window.

Smooth stones, shells,
          and something, something
that will be memorized by the heart.

Waiting for Annie

I lie awake,
A windy night—
The moon travels
In slow motion.
A nameless thing
Takes me in.

Sleeping alone
Curled in blue light,
I get up to walk
And come to the window,
Bare feet on cold wood floor.

A whisper, a turn,
Settling in,
Into the night—
Across the bay
Beach grass rocks
In night wind.

St. Valentine's Day

Mica comes to the daycare door out of breath
in her red dress.
Presents me with a cardboard heart.
For her it has been a long afternoon
of fish, kites, whistling herons,
boats on the rising moon.

For me, the red heart brings a remembered heat
of a slow brewing storm, and that drab time
between winter and winter.

She says, *remember, mama, fish can fly.*
We take ourselves home,
followed by a spring dragon kite.

Wings of light shimmer off the red heart
placed carefully in the window of our house.

Orca Inlet

Metal roofs shine with the rain of Cordova,
grey, green, silver-blue.
Across the bay, the green-treed island,
Hawkins, shrouded with mist, low lying fog.
It creeps into town, hangs from the trees,
slinks down streets,
envelopes this house from all corners.

Boats are at the business of catching salmon.
In the Sound, pinks, reds, kings, silvers;
nets, lead line, cork.
The set must be just right.
The purse seine draws in and holds the many silvered fish.
Another set and another,
until the night closes down around the boats.

Soon planes will circle like hawks and spot fish
for the next time around, and around the island in the
waiting town.
The women wait
and wait for the boats to return to the harbor.

They recite to themselves a litany of names—
Siren, Seafever, Sunrunner
Towhee, Murelette, Kittiwake....

Gulls craze near the canneries.
Sun gleams on the water, and soon
the boats begin coming in,
leaving a wide trail of wake water
like a long soft veil.

Icarus Dreams

The sky is too near.
We circle and glide,
two seabirds
over gray waves.

The direction I face holds you.
Entangled in your own dream,
you invite me in. I stop the task
of netting in the ordinary days
to begin day like no other, etched in.

Like night spiders we spin these
intricate structures, bridges, frail
and moving ever so slightly
in morning mist.

Renewed, I mouth: here I am.
But that is not me.
I am this person who—but
that is not me.

Impossible to measure up to this
terrible gift,
to live up to words
that turn to so many brown leaves
surrounding our bed in the morning.

I hear the seasound
from far, far off.
In your voice is your voice,
the seasound, echo.

Last Day in Town

This night and this night
and this night the snow is heavy.
We pull the baby bundled in the red sled
over the quiet streets
to the inn for a hot drink.

This town feels so right and easy
to move around in—
like home yet not home.

It was the closeness
the rain
could circle round, draw up
and catch you right off guard.

Well, it's our last day in town.
We were thinking these thoughts.
We were thinking these things.

The grave of our dog
is now grown over with soft green moss
and the stone is white and round.

II. China

We shall not cease from exploration, and the end of all our exploring will be to arrive where we started and know the place for the first time.
—T.S. Eliot, *Little Gidding*

Slender Joy

Sappho calls love "fiction weaving."
Socrates names love the wizard.

She calls it the white space
between every thought,

the pen you write with,
the song you sing,
that unexpected kiss,
the book you read from,
the wind in your hair,

as you ride your black bicycle
down the road
to your house,

where roses bloom in November
and the slender moon comes in
through the window.

Red

Red is not blood.
Is not passion.
Is not anger.
Red is ancient.
Red is secret.
Red is the poet's red.
Red is wine.
Red is sex.
Red are the roses you hang
in the kitchen to dry.
The rug we lie on.

A child's knotted hat
with black braids
hanging down.

Red is the inner courtyard,
the wall of forbidden cities.

Red is the sound
of many voices
crying out in the square,
ghosts of red.

This Message

When you see Mr. Gao,
please give him these photographs.
Tell him I'm sorry
that he stopped coming around.

And tell him to find
his own way
in this world
without leaning on a woman.
When he learns to stand up tall,
he will stop being afraid.

I miss his voice.
But I have his silence.
A land of no words
is a strange place.
There are walls, even doors,
but no windows
for the moon to come in.

When you see him,
please tell him
I was happy
on the nights we were together.
Tell him I remembered
my body
after a long time
of not remembering.
Tell him
it was a winter storm
on the ocean.
Tell him that.

Pictures at an Exhibition

Yes, we went together to many exhibitions,
both local and international: Rodin, Chagall,
I remember particularly well.

When we went together,
we would look and then tell each our favorites.
Often they were the same sculptures or paintings.
Police would cancel an exhibition
at the last minute for any reason.
They censored anything remotely sexual or political.

Usually it was some Chinese artist,
not the big names,
who were more acceptable worldwide.

Concerts of music, exhibitions of paintings,
poetry readings were unheard of.
Not broadcast but held in someone's home,
spur of the moment.
I held a reading on a Sunday afternoon—
Father's Day.
A Chinese poet asked me
if I would read "Daddy" by Sylvia Plath.
I was honored.

Later that night I got sick
and passed out in the bathroom.
I was alone.
Remember asking someone to help me
and then I fainted and fell on the floor,
hitting my head on the bathroom sink.

You knew something was wrong
and you showed concern.
Yes, Vincent, you were always there for me.
Yes, always.

Bamboo in the Moonlight

All day I look at those Chinese paintings.
Tonight I lay out my brushes.
the stone, ink and paper.

Tomorrow I may begin.

Night Watch, Mid-Autumn

Listen—
Crickets chirping—
    Full moon—
        And me without any wine.

The Disappearing Gardener

Our gardener, a tall Chinese
with a gravelly Northern accent,
always wears a long blue coat
in summer and winter,
keeps his ears warm
under a hat with flaps.
He looks like a big puppy.

He tends the square of bare earth,
armed with a rake, often a wheelbarrow,
carts off the day's finds:
a pair of tennis shoes,
some foreign magazines,
a cast off suitcase ....

Outside the wall
early morning figures practice
t'ai chi, sword dances,
calligraphy shadows.
Nearby, two magpies
build their nest
(surely a sign of good luck).

And beyond, across the road,
winter cabbages are stacked on balconies;
an old man releases his pigeons
twice a day.

Retired men in grey Mao jackets
bicycle to the park,
exercise their pet birds
in bamboo cages,

intent on training the meadowlarks
to compete for the sweetest melody.

Our gardener doesn't imagine
he lives in our barbarian hearts.
One night we stay up by candlelight,
cover the floor of our foreigner apartment,
drawing, painting his image,
an ordinary Chinese man
whose life is unknowable to us.

Shi Yan (Stone Mountain)

Don't talk back, Stone.
You're making the bird sellers angry,
trying to get a cheaper price.
Just stop your haggling;
pay the man.
He knows you are with me,
a foreigner with money,
so we must pay and leave.

It's not about saving face.
It's your anger at everything else,
spilling out.
The lack of possible suitors,
and you, now 27, too old
to be single in the middle kingdom.

You, a strong Chinese woman,
educated at Bei Da.
After Tiananmen,
witness to the spirited youth
crushed by old men,
playing emperor,
only to be forced
to work in the fields.
To be re-educated,
to almost have died there
under those harsh ways.

You say you want to go abroad?
Enjoy all things Western?
You speak perfect English,
have ambitions to be the next Connie Chung.

I've watched you drink all the men under the table.
I adopt you as my long-lost daughter.
We stay up way into the night, girl talk.

And then one day
you betray me
in that deceitful web
when brother spied upon brother.
friend turned in friend,
a leftover remnant from the Days of Chaos,
the Cultural Revolution,
reporting me to the authorities.
I'm made to write a self-criticism.
(Spiritual pollution is my crime.)

Stone, how can I ever trust you again?

Sneaking Past the Guards at the Gate of Bei Wei

They're asleep with their heads on the table.
It's four a.m. and we sneak past them
to fall into our beds after a night
of drinking whiskey and dancing at the night clubs.

Sneaking in my Chinese lover past the *fu yuans*
in the Foreign Exchange Building,
We are committing a political act.
We climb in the window
past the blooming roses of November,
The full moon witness to our crime.

Four Postcards in Black and White

This Chinese character means graceful, intelligent,
beautiful, elegant.
I practice writing the character
until it releases its meaning—*xiu*.

This postcard is a dream.
A white bird carries your letter
across the ocean, lets it drop far below
while it disappears into the waves.

And then this one—
figures skate on a city pond—
New York, 1940. I write to you
in the back of a taxi, my hands
numb with cold.
It's a long way from summer.

An hour's train ride from Paris—
I begin to write *topaz*...
then cross out the words,
write over and over them,

line your postcard in black
to tell you
I have passed into winter
into the strong black strokes
of Chinese characters—fluid ink
upon white rice paper.

Dear Ghost-Person

Dear Ghost-Person,
I must have dreamed our connection,
that slim, brief communion of love.
Small details help me remember.

Nothing replaces the absence of you.
If I could bring you here,
but you are no commodity,
no import-export trade quota.
And there are no easy answers.

Again green—
the trees line,
the American Embassy in Beijing—
the hopefuls wait patiently,
to be accepted
or turned away.

We drink beer at the edge of the lake,
and sit side by side until everyone leaves,
not talking, just being.
Behind us
the trees bloom in the night,
glowing.

Each morning on my drive to work
I pray for another
moment of clarity—like the time
we met in the middle of the road
and all things fell away,
everything went white with light,
and we both knew what we wanted.

Wind

You sweep in from Mongolia
into the gritty streets
of this small village.

You are my friend
my enemy,
my secret lover.

You come and go
on your own.
I have no control
over your coming
and going.

You take away
my words—
I am breathless,
mute.

You stir up trouble
for a day or two.

When I wake in the morning
you are gone.
All is clear—
all is light
and I am
transparent
as glass.

III. Pacific Northwest

When we returned from the immersion—
how sweet, how deep.
                    —Virginia Woolf, *The Waves*

To the Woman with the Top of Her Head Missing

after a sculpture by Judith Hill

The ancient horse you ride
has no eyes.
The top of your head is missing.
In your hand a carrot
carried like a sword.

Woman, always going into battle,
consider what you have already lost.
Or consider what might be gained
beyond, if you continue your search—

eyes, brains, the top of your head,
or a land of no color,
a circle of stones,
a forest without trees.

Women Picking Blackberries

We trade summer's end.
I bring you roses, one of each—
Wise Portia, Shadow Dancer,
Sophy's Rose, Mary Rose.

And a basket of garden tomatoes
ripe and ready for eating.

You show me the best spots
for Himalayan blackberries,
lush for eating.

And Century pears,
a whole bucket of them
ready for eating.

Roses for blackberries,
tomatoes for pears—
summer's full circle
comes to an end.

We talk as we pick,
caution each other not to overreach,
fall into the brambles.

I tell you about old women's bodies
at the swimming pool,
unselfconscious, lovely,
like these blackberries,
the full September roses,
red tomatoes, Asian pears.

At the Oceanview Cemetery in Port Angeles

Raymond Carver May 25, 1938—August 2, 1992,
Tess July 21,1943—

She walks over to the cliff
And throws the old flowers
Over the side.

Tess, with her long dark hair,
A big rose on her black hat,
Splash of bright color,

The ocean.
Crows caw,
Raucous and disrespectful.

We sit off to the side,
And watch while she cleans
The black granite with Windex, paper towels,

Sets out a new bouquet of wildflowers.
Indian paintbrush, chocolate lilies,
Daisies, yellow columbine.

The last sound of a car door shutting
In that silent place,
As she drives off in his old, grey Mercedes.

Poem in My Husband's Notebook

Dear man I married—
here's your pain on a platter,

here's your head in my lap,
here's your "sorry,

I'm not feeling well again"
in my head.

We are two ancients,
trapped in bodies without wings.

Pulling Dandelions

Because they are weeds.
Because I like my lawn green.
Because I don't use Round Up.
Because it gets me outside.
Because I like my made-in-England digger.
Because I am a gardener.
Because good gardeners kill plants.
Because I like the satisfying *pop* when I dig roots and all.
Because it's a challenge.
Because I must.

Mid-November

Imagine
you are riding a ferryboat
in the Pacific Northwest.
It is night and the ferry
is lit up like a birthday cake,
one that glides magically
across ink smooth waters.

The boat hums and moves
like a shadow
through your imagination.
Underneath your feet,
below the car deck,
salmon and seals
live in their watery world.

Imagine
you are coming to meet
this woman
after seasons
heavy with the silence
of two separate lives.
You arrive at the end
of the ferry ride
and walk off with the
other passengers, some locals,
some Canadians, some from far away,
like you.

Imagine
the woman standing
at the dock

waiting for you,
a long green coat,
black scarf,
and a sign,
like they use in China,
a sign on a stick,
only not your name,
but this painting:

a sun eclipsed
by the black moon,
Mars and Aries,
the numbers 123,
and the Statue of Liberty
and a small red flag
with gold stars.

Imagine
the woman holding this sign
meant to greet you.
She understands your language
in a world where no one
speaks to you,
but where all things
are possible.

Last Week

Last week
on the ferry
I saw a view
of water, trees,
the whole range
of Cascade mountains.
Like a framed painting
I wanted to give you
this vista,
this long view
of my life.

For a moment
then
I thought
you might
want this too.
This northwestern view
of blue and green
and greys,
low lying clouds
touching the tips
of evergreens,
a heron
frozen still
at the water's edge
near the lights
of the ferry dock.

Water separates us
and draws us together.
We must travel the

great bodies of water
that mark the boundaries
of our two countries.
When the wind blows here
I wonder if the wind blows there.
When the days grow brief,
with fading light,
I wonder if you too
have these brief days.

How much distance
do we allow
before the seasons
wrap themselves
around us like a shroud,
before the flower bulbs
I planted in the ground
wait in the dark
for something eternal,
something bright and new.

Where I Want to Be

Low tide on a beach
and that familiar sound
of water washing over beach stones
that tells me
go back, go back, go back ....

Woman of sun, woman of water.
I am one of those beach stones
you kick up with your feet.
I am one of the marauding
glaucous winged gulls.
I am the intense heat of the sun,
so strong I burn out your eyes.
You could die without water.

Tomorrow, a lizard,
a new-found hollowed out bowl.
Empty. Ready to be received.

Gift from Port Townsend

I'm looking for something to take home
For my child

Gull feather
Motion of the waves

Wide and open sky

A pair of mergansers in flight

The rocking, rocking bay waters
Are the lullaby I sing

When I see her she may not remember me

Does she dream of my hands
On her back
Sending her to sleep?

Seattle, Night Driving

Rain, neon, jazz—
Comfortable car boxes me in—
No one knows me here.
I drive with the ease
of one with no past,
no destination.

I drive these familiar streets
late at night, the windshield wipers swishing
gray mist away every 30 seconds
into an arc of sudden clarity.
Then the night hazes into neon
wavering and shimmering
off the black pavement.

Jazz, Mingus—
A woman sings, blue,
at the inattention of her lover.

That woman should try driving.
It could pull her out of her man-slump.
Men—what good are they?
They want to take away
our power steering,
the car keys, say "Stay at home,
with the children, the dog, your knitting.
I'm going out.'"

Hey, honey,
sometimes my car wants to run
off the road at high speed
on dangerous mountain passes.

I stay in the far lane
tempting gravity.

But look,
this driving is like writing.
Everything is neat, crisp,
usually goes smoothly.
Just follow the rules—
turn here, brake slowly,
accelerate, shift gears,
merge, yield.

Don't Move

This time
this morning
this light;
you are bathed
in this golden light;
the slow sound of the ocean
below us in our beach house
wave after wave after wave.

Pine tree scent
tea and oranges
and grapefruit
wild blackberries for picking
in our crow yard.

I say
don't move
don't move
submit, surrender,
let me do it all;
don't move
over and over
like the waves
below us.

I lie on the sand
with eyes closed,
throw back my head
to the sun,

and remember
how we soared

and came and died
and became each other.
No you or I, not even an us,
just the stars and the waves.

Never Turn Your Back on the Ocean

Consider this world
this place we find ourselves in
the long hours of pleasure
of discovering the dark and the new.

Consider how time stops for us
when we are touching.
All time stops in this way.

Consider how the strongest element, water,
takes us to the place we need to go;
the sound of the rushing stream at night
in our flashlight walk through the forest.
If I stand there long enough
next to that sound of the waterfall,
I am above you, about
the tree branches, looking down.
Look up. Look up from us.

This pattern tells me
that all things are possible.
Under the lacework, all loneliness leaves,
all emptiness fills.
When we stand with our backs to the ocean,
daring the rolling waves to take us with them,
submerged, under all that intensity,
when we rise we can only exhale.

My Muse Left Town Today

My muse left town today.
There she goes on the ferry boat
crossing the water;
leaving me behind
to attend to all the details
of my stupid little life.

My muse left town today.
I watch her leave on the ferry,
across Guemes Channel.
It's only a ten-minute crossing
but already I feel so sad and blue.

Docking at the other side
my muse leaves me
to wander about.

What I can do here in this
white house by the sea

with Willow and Sophie,
the lazy cats,
too fat from winter's sleep
and lack of bird and mouse activity.
So they sleep through the day
curled up on the sofa
or the leather chair,
sleep and dream of more birds and mice.
Food from the can,
the sound of their own quiet breath.

I am trying to be balanced,
but you see, my muse left me.
Out of town, no cell phone to reach her,
to get her back
and safely back, too.
Wait! Here comes the return boat!
with cars and raincoated passengers.
Maybe she's changed her mind.
Maybe I can coax her into the house
with some hot cocoa or a wood fire.

I will open my arms,
wait by the front door.
Quietly, I will wait
until the words start glowing
through these fingers
and onto the page.

Along with the bright morning sun,
she crosses over the blue ribbon of water
through the fog-ridden air,
to return to the waiting poet,
the woman who paces
from restless room to room.
Waiting the return of that hot white space
where all the nameless things of the world
take shape.

IV. People and Other Places

Let reason flow like water around a stone,
the stone remains.
                    —Jane Hirshfield, *Come, Thief*

Riding the Creek Road, Heartland

Riding the creek road
Circular spoke motion
This is where it all began.
Alabaster creek music
Birdsong
Farmers' fields
Ancient eyes of cows
Sleeping cat on porch
This road on bicycle
Heartland
Where it all began.

Classic Red

The lipstick makes her remember
evenings her mother would go out,
Saturday nights, dancing with her father.
Then she thought her mother was the most
beautiful woman in the world.
Then she wanted to grow up like her:
clip-on pearl earrings, high heels, and
lipstick, a deep red blood.

The Breadman's Daughter

At night I hear the ballgame.
June bugs buzz against the screen door,
hum of florescent kitchen light.
Everyone else sleeps.
Our silence sits at the table with us.
Some things are never mentioned.
Most of our conversations remain
somewhere inside that red plastic radio.

A robin sings out in his night perch.
Downstairs I hear you rise and imagine you
as you start up the bread truck;
it's four a.m.—
starched shirt, gray pants, striped tie.
Another workday begins
with its chorus of robins in the maples
as I turn in my bed upstairs
and fall back to sleep.

There it is. The white cup;
filled with pennies for milk money.
Mother stands at the ironing board
with the sprinkler for your shirts.
This was the order of our lives then.

On the coldest days you drive us to school
and we ride up front, all of us standing,
leaning into the racks, which hold the
fragrant bread.

Letter to My Sister

Suppose we saw that room now,
A room of sun and light. We climb to
The attic bedroom of the farmhouse.
There are things I remember:
Wind up the phonograph,
Marble top dresser
Aunt Anne's long blue formal.
Long winter nights of flannel
And dressing under covers.
A bed where once at night
We heard wolves howling.

After years of sharing the bedroom,
We could each have our own island.
Paper the walls a cornflower blue.
Paint the trim white,
Line walls with books.
Bed neatly made.

If I Let Myself

If I let myself
Grow quiet
I can almost imagine
My life at age ten
When fall leaves
Burned sweet leaf smoke
And there were no dark secrets.

Landed Immigrant, Nova Scotia

Driving the line of the Canadian villages:
Short Beach, Port Maitland, Wellington,
some French, some British;
We reach McCormack Road
and the 200-year-old farmhouse,
our new home.
Every room painted pale lavender,
Second floor gallery of old photographs
stare down at us. We close off rooms
to save heat and sleep
in the front downstairs bedroom
known as the "dying room."

In Wellington
women meet once a month
in their farmhouses down the road.
Their houses shine. They invite me,
a Yankee, to a meeting. In the kitchens they have
sleek black oil and wood cook stoves.
My year-old daughter bounces on my knee.

A singing wind encircles the outbuildings,
silver and never ending, it polishes the green car
with beach sand and sighs.
Laundry stiffens outside
frozen in misshapen bodies.

My main job is to keep the wood fires burning,
and to entertain 90-year-old Uncle John
who lives up the road with relatives
with coffee and a homemade pie.

In the pig barn,
pencil scratches on the beams tell of past lives:
number of pigs, sold, slaughtered,
an unusually cold winter,
cords of wood sold from neighbor's lot.

At dusk peepers predict
the coming of a new season.
We wait for our immigration papers,
wonder who will write from home.

One June Night

One June Sunday in the Stone House
in Shaftsbury, Vermont, I was standing
in the front room, the same room
where Robert Lee Frost composed
"Stopping by Woods on a Snowy Evening"
in the 1920s on a hot June evening.

I witnessed a glimmer of the man,
with his wild hair
and faded blue bathrobe,
heading toward the dawning light
to get some needed air
after working the poem all night long.

I watched the shadow of him leave that room,
crossing the wide pine plank floor
to go outside for a moment,
and with staying up the whole night,
then to marvel at the light in the blooming lilacs
that small detail, that one moment
where form, meter, rhyme,
all fall into perfect place.

Laughing in Your Sleep

Hey there, you,
it's been years since you've
unselfconsciously laughed out loud
in your sleep.
Why is that?

What strange grey cloud
has settled over you,
that you no longer
chuckle or chortle and yes,
even snort
in your dreams?

You used to wake me
that way,
and I'd say
what's so funny
and you'd tell me
some snippet
of a poppet dream,
some nonesuch nonsense.

And now you sit across from me
on this veranda
in Mexico,
reading the book I gave you
for the trip,
about an Irish guy named McCarthy,
and you laugh out loud,
sniggle-dee-dee
and sure, I am glad
for your laughter.

Boundary Line

Our neighbor has a brain tumor.
What does he think about,
his time left on earth?

I leaf through
garden catalogues
hungry for green.

I order bareroot roses:
William Shakespeare,
Falstaff, Wise Portia.

Forsythia blossoms
bright yellow
between our houses.

He cuts back our hydrangea,
the flowering quince,
plans to erect a chain link fence.

He probably won't live to see the roses
hanging over the property line
in full red bloom.

Provence, Here is Where I Belong

Saint, heretic, witch, druid, crusader ...

Certainly I am from this place

of stone and mountains,
of heat and *cigales*,
sun and lavender,

all the wild colors that drove
Van Gogh mad.

The Margarita Poems

I. (One-minute poem composed at Mexican restaurant, El Jinete,
Anacortes)

I'll write something
if you insist.
I'll pull myself away
from the salsa and chips,
from the hand on my shoulder,
the Muzak in the background.
I'll write the goddamn poem,
but I won't be happy about it.

II. (Eavesdropping Again)

I don't hear the music
like you do.
I hear, or overhear voices
from the nearby booths
and catch snatches
of conversation.
I eavesdrop at restaurants.
Always listening
for that perfectly tuned phrase,
the one I imagined in my sleep.

III. (This Poem is called Anticipation)

I don't want to write anymore.
You write. All right.

My handwriting sprawls
across the page;

sometimes words fall off the edge,
misjudged the space and distance again,
like my balance when I walk.
I may not be the person you think I am.
I may just evaporate into the night air,
join the billions and billions of stars
in this vast universe.

Promise me you'll
make love to me again tonight.

IV. (Mango or Mambo?)

Salt—lots of it,
On the rocks, of course.
Tequila makes me crazy.
Lime juice—fresh—
your house special.
Margarita, please.
Just one.
We have to walk home.

Conversation Between the Artist and Me

after the painting Patchwork—Ghost Ranch by Maggie Muchmore, Santa Fe,
NM

What would I ask you?
I am interested in how you view this landscape,
my favorite place in the whole state.
You've got the colors right:
rojo, amarillo, ochre.
Ancient hills and mountains,
azul sky,
so blue you can get lost in it.

Imagine the song birds—
canyon wren, trilling downward,
or that curve billed thrasher
hopping in the *cholla.*
See the raven glide
like a smooth calligraphy shadow.

Azul sky—
I am hiking in the back country.
My two golden retrievers run free.
My legs carry me.
I have water, my notebook,
and all this silence.

Salt of the Earth

after the photograph by Sebastiao Salgado

His eyes tell many stories,
of poverty, want, neglect,
dignity, grace, intelligence.

He is not smiling,
but looking straight into the camera.
His black hair, parted down the middle,
looks like two blackbirds taking flight.
Imagine a long braid down his back.

A blank wall behind him,
he stands in a doorway, one hand
strong and curled in itself.

He is not old, not young.
He could be a musician, a priest,
a shepherd, a city-dweller,
an Ecuadorian prince.

My eyes keep searching his eyes.
The life he's led, his life in front of him.

To his left stands a smaller, mysterious figure:
male, female, old, young, a figure
turned away from us covered
in black cloak, a wide-brimmed hat.

Anonymous people tell us everything
and nothing. They could be lovers
or strangers or both.

Suicide Drawing

after the drawing *Many Worlds Interpretation* by James Drake

He's a pothole patcher on the road of love.
                    —Jimmy Santiago Baca

Contemplate doing yourself in—
who had not done this before?
Consider the word itself; like
cyanide, pesticide, infanticide—
A sin, you have taken your own life.
Left a mess for someone else to clean up;
you will not be buried with the Christian souls,
but on the other side of the cemetery fence,
with the unsaved, the heathens.

Guns, pills, poison, hanging, car exhaust, slit wrists,
or jumping off the back of a boat,
or walking into a river
weighed down by rocks in your pockets.
We know all the sordid details;
any way to end the pain, the desolation, the dark,
the opposite of living, you choose to end it all.
Are you a brave soul or a coward?
Are you glad to have made this plan?

A Story

The women had to bend.
The women were told to be silent
while the magnificent gleaming tiger
patrolled the roads.
The women were kept inside
a tiny hut
no bigger than a pocket.
When the snow fell, bright and new,
the women asked to go out
but were kept back,
told it would be too
dangerous.

The light was diffused.
The pine trees guarded their secrets.

Ancestors

We thought it might be cancer.
We thought it was terminal.

Your death
a short-lived rose
gone petal by petal
until only the soft middle
of memory stays behind.

Your death
like so many crypts
inches skyward,
light bent to take in
a stone angel's gaze.

Women Who

Women with thickening waists.
Women with drooping breasts.
Women with fat ankles.
Wrinkles
Blotchy skin
thinning hair.
Women who shop
without finding
any elegant clothes.
Women who handle
their own finances.
Who maintain their cars,
laptops,
the vacuum cleaner.
Women who
live alone.
Women who
like living alone.
Women who
don't buy *Vogue*
anymore.
Women who
hum to themselves
in the grocery store line.
Women who
are no longer angry.
Women whose
favorite companions
are their cats.
Women who like dogs
better than men.
Women who

are witches.
Women who
grow old.
Women who
love their absent children.
Women who
bury their parents.
Women who
are grandmothers.
Women who
live on the streets.
Women who
forget their
own address.
Women who
are invisible.
Women who
no longer
wear bright colors.
Women who
always wear black.
Women who
mourn.
Women who
forgive their past.

The Things She Left

the oranges
and the skirts in the closet
the keys on the table
and her reflection above them
the far away singing
and the color green
the weight of the bedcovers
and the late night cooking
the book on the nightstand

Swimming Without Fear

This is how the night fell.
There was a light from the lake.
The stir of night creatures:
bats, crickets, a croaking frog.
It came down like a curtain,
this night of clarity.

I could not go inside.
I walked through the pines, the Douglas firs,
to the deep lake
and then I became part of the night,
the night that summer ended
and the quiet began.

Like fall arriving on a Tuesday,
I wanted to see the green heron.
No one wished me happiness.
I asked you what reasons
stood in the way of our loving
one another.

Into the lake
I am covered by the moon's
path. I swim without fear.
Like a white glove,
the moon carries me.
I was there.
I was the night.

About the Author

Poet and painter Alice Lee (aliceroselee.com) is the former editor and publisher of the Alaskan letterpress publishing house Orca Press, for which she received a Pushcart Prize for best of the small presses. She was also editor and publisher for Whistle Lake Press in Washington. Lee was an Alaskan Poet Laureate finalist and has been awarded artist residencies at Yaddo, Hedgebrook, Villa Montalvo (California) and Avignon, France. She taught college English for 30-plus years in Missouri, Alaska, Seattle, China and Whidbey Island, Washington.

Lee's poems have appeared in *Alaska Quarterly Review, Calyx, Kansas Quarterly, San Francisco Poetry Review, New Mexico Poetry Review, Blue Mesa, Adobe Walls,* and other publications. She has held solo shows of her art in the U.S. and abroad.

Besides writing and painting, Lee enjoys reading, travel, gardening, and films. She lives with her poet husband Wayne Lee in Portland, Oregon.